THE TRUE STEEL RAIL

FOR RAILWAYS.

BOOTH'S PATENT

STEEL TREAD,

DUPLEX STEEL AND IRON RAILS

FOR RAILWAYS.

THEIR MANUFACTURE

EXPLAINED, AND MERITS DISCUSSED.

NEW EDITION.

J. L. BOOTH,

Patentee and Manufacturer,

ROCHESTER, N. Y.

ROCHESTER, N. Y.

BENTON AND ANDREWS, BOOK AND JOB PRINTERS.

1868.

STEEL TREAD,

DUPLEX STEEL AND IRON RAILS,

FOR RAILWAYS.

The above cut represents a transverse section of the Steel Capped Rail, now manufactured by the Patentee for the New York Central Rail-Road Company, and others. The form has been carefully studied, and is believed to be the best attainable, being four inches wide at flange, four inches high, and a good width of cap—two and one-half inches.

The weight of the rail, as now manufactured, is 59 pounds to the yard—in the proportion of 15 pounds steel and 44 pounds iron. These proportions may be varied to any extent, at the pleasure of the purchaser, the price differing accordingly. We are now prepared to furnish this rail in any quantity ordered. The steel cap will never become loose, and the rail will be equal in wear to solid steel, and in other respects, far preferable.

Description of the Rail.

It will be seen at a glance, that the rail consists of an iron base with a steel cap, united to the base, not by bolts, screws or rivets, but simply by clamping. The iron bar is rolled at the required form and weight, after which the steel cap, having been rolled of the proper form and length, is properly tempered and placed upon the cold iron base. The two are then passed through the Compressing machine, which presses the cap down upon the base and clenches in its side. A good fit and a fast hold are thus obtained, with a powerful shrinkage.

To remove the steel cap for refitting or other purposes, the iron base is firmly secured, and by a hook on each side of the cap a separation is formed at one end, and followed through by rolls the entire length of the rail.

New Features of the Invention.

Patents have been obtained upon this rail in the United States, Great Britain, France and Belgium. By the original patents there is secured to the inventor the sole and exclusive right to manufacture, use and sell rails, composed of the iron body and steel cap, when the latter is rolled and shrunk on the body in such a manner as to unite the parts closely as a unit or whole, but still allow them to be easily separated and replaced. More recent patents secure the use of the combination of the cap and base, with depressions or indentations in the base, as found desirable.

This feature of clamping the cap around the head of the iron base, is thus recognized by the Patent Office as a new and original feature. Other compound rails have been made of iron and steel, but in all cases the steel and iron have been united by rivets, bolts or welding. These have all proved defective. Besides other causes of displacement, the variation in climate of 125 degrees annually, expanding and contracting the iron and steel differently, has been found sufficient to cut off the rivets and tear asunder the welding. Booth's arrangement obviates this difficulty entirely, by allowing the cap to slide sufficiently on the rail without displacement or injury to either material.

Utility of the Invention.

In this form of rail, are combined, it is believed, all the advantages of both iron and steel rails, with others that would alone render it superior to either. Notwithstanding the prevailing tendency to extol the merits of the steel rail, there is no doubt that the iron rail possesses some obvious advantages over its rival, and further experience of steel may show that it has others. Its obvious advantages are:

1. Cheapness in first cost.
2. Greater elasticity under travel.
3. Capability of being made over.

To offset these, there is claimed for steel rails so much greater durability as alone to render them more economical on the whole; but whether this will prove to be the fact in view of their special disadvantages, can only be determined by experience. These disadvantages are:

1. Greater first cost.
2. Greater rigidity under work.
3. Liability to break.
4. Incapability of being made over.

The 1st and 4th of these disadvantages are of obvious weight in the consideration of economy. The extent of bearing of the 2d and 3d cannot at present be accurately estimated. There can be little doubt, however, that the greater rigidity of the rail (which is apparent, even to the traveler over it, by the harsh and disagreeable grating sensation it produces) depreciates the rolling stock more rapidly. The granite ties or stone work upon which railways were first laid, are, for this cause, now universally discontinued. With regard to the breakage of steel rails, we have some evidence furnished in a late report of the President of the Michigan Central Rail-Road Company, James F. Joy. He says (see Report, 1868, page 7):

"Three miles of steel rails have been laid, and thus far they have hardly borne the test, having been found more liable to break than iron."

These rails are of the best English made Bessemer steel. Also, in the report for 1868, of the President of the Chicago B. & Q. R. R. He says:

"We have laid about three miles of steel rails where they will be subject to the greatest wear, in order to test their quality and durability, as compared with iron. The result thus far has not been such as to encourage the Board in an extended use of it in the ordinary track of the road."

Thus it appears that the only certain advantage that the steel rail possesses over the iron, is its greater durability.

Our next inquiry will be to compare the Booth Rail with both the others, in respect to the qualities above considered:

1st, Cost.—The first Cost of the Booth rail is much less than that of steel, though of course, greater than iron. But it has been suggested that *in case* steel should be hereafter made as cheap as iron, that this advantage would be lost. We contend, however, that even in such an improbable event, the Booth rail could still be made cheaper than the steel, inasmuch as vast quantities of old iron rail, from which it could be made, would then be inevitably on the market, at prices much below their usual standard of value. This can be worked over into the iron base of the Booth rail, and the whole rail thus be made at a less cost than steel rails from new material.

2d, Durability.—Supposing the cap to remain firmly in its place (a point which we shall consider hereafter), it is evident that it will wear as well and as long as any other steel surface. The thickness of the cap being about one-half an inch (and more if desired), it will only wear out by the same abrasion of surface as would render a solid steel rail useless, especially as this abrasion would not be uniform but irregular. The *first* wear of this rail, therefore, will be equal to that of the steel rail. What that wear would be, may perhaps be pretty nearly estimated. English experience establishes the fact that a steel rail will outwear seventeen iron rails in the same service. It is also stated that it takes eleven million wheels to reduce a steel head seven pounds to the yard—there being no lamination, but a uniform wearing away, as by friction. If these reports are true, it would take forty years to reduce seven pounds to the yard, upon the straight portion of any principal railway in the United States.

The Booth rail, as now made, has fifteen pounds steel to the yard, and after a uniform reduction of seven pounds to the yard, it would still be serviceable.

In point of exemption from liability to breakage, it is evident that its advantages are at least equal to that of the iron and therefore, as we shall prove hereafter, superior (in all probability) to steel. We are now considering economy merely in the light of the durability (or life) of the rail. But this exemption from liability to breakage has a more important bearing on the question of economy, by its result in freedom from accident. And we shall, therefore, examine the subject further, when we come to consider the special advantages of the Booth rail, with reference to safety.

3d, Capability of being worked over.—In this respect the Booth rail enjoys a great superiority. The steel rail once discarded, is useless; and even the iron rail must be taken to a distant rolling mill, and re-rolled at great expense. But the Booth rail can, by machinery that will not cost over $15,000, and which every Rail Road Company can afford to own, be at once re-capped, at a comparatively small expense.

4th, Elasticity under travel.—The base of the Booth rail being of iron, exhibits the same advantage in this respect as an iron rail. The extent of this advantage in its effect upon the wear of rolling stock, as well as upon the comfort of the traveling public, we have before suggested, can only be fully ascertained by experience. When it is remembered that the steel rails in use are three times as stiff between ties as iron, it will be apparent that the effect of this increased rigidity *may be* considerable, and the advantage of an iron base is, therefore, well worthy of consideration.

Other special advantages—Safety.—It thus appears that the Booth rail possesses the combined advantages of both the simple rails, and that in the important quality of economy, it is far superior to either. It is also superior to either in the no less important quality of *safety*, for being a duplex rail it cannot break unless flaws in both parts should come together, which is to the last degree improbable. Hence either part may break, without danger of immediate accident, giving an opportunity to substitute a sound for the broken rail. The numerous accidents, some frightful and all expensive, that have occurred during the last few years, from broken rails, will attract to this advantage of the Booth rail, a serious attention.

It would seem that the steel rails are more liable to breakage than iron. Much skill is required in their manufacture, and there is thus more danger of flaws, or burning, or imperfect temper. Many have, in fact, broken from being made too hard, and it is certain that in casting the ingot of Bessemer steel, many crack transversely. These flaws, in many cases, even if extending half through a piece of steel (sixty pounds to the yard), would hardly be discovered, even by a sledge-hammer test. Yet with a forty ton engine, on a cold night, there would too probably be a different result. Flaws might also occur, and undoubtedly do, in the Booth steel cap, but as this weighs only fifteen or sixteen pounds to the yard, the test of the hammer, which is always applied before its application to the rail, and the further test secured by the process of rolling on the cap, are sure to discover the defect, and even should these both fail, there is, as already observed, an additional security in the strength of the iron base. It is a well know fact that iron and steel united, cannot be broken as easily as the same size piece of either separately.

In this connection we may add that the strength of this rail has been practically tested in comparison with iron and steel rails of the same weight, under a powerful press, and shows a marked superiority over both. Attempts to break it by repeatedly bending it in opposite directions, proved unavailing.

Facility of Repair.

We have already shown that any Rail-Road Company can take up and repair its own rails, at moderate expense, but there is more to be said on this subject. In case a rail fails to wear evenly, or become battered or defaced at the ends, there is no need of losing it like an iron or steel rail, or even of taking it up, but the defaced portion can be at once cut out by means of a milling tool, and the rail re-capped in that part without removal.

Economy.

In considering first cost, durability, capability of repair and safety, we have already discussed the question of economy to some extent, but a word or two further may be admissible. For should the iron base of the Booth rail ever become so worn as to be worthless, except for working over (which it certainly will not do *sooner* than a solid steel rail would), it will then be marketable, which the steel rail would not, at least to the same extent.

It is doubtful whether old steel rails could be sold to-day for $40 per ton, if at all, but *old iron rails are always marketable*, and the iron base of the Booth rail, delivered at the capping mill, will be always worth (at present standard of prices), say $65 to $70 per ton. Thus we show a rail intrinsically worth, all things considered, at least $50 per ton *more* than a solid steel rail, and yet furnished to the consumer at a much less price. With these suggestions we think it unnecessary to discuss the question of economy further.

Will the Cap remain Firm?

This obvious question of the first importance, requires to be answered, and to it we will now give our attention. The inventor's theory was, that the cap would become *tighter* by use, owing to the expansion of the upper surface under travel to a greater extent than the surface next the rail. The process is that known by mechanics as "peaning," and may be illustrated by the following cut.

The figure represents a straight bar of iron, which having been laid upon a curved surface, will by a succession of light blows upon the upper surface, be thrown into a curve form represented by the dotted line. This is a well known effect, and we venture to say there is no force or power employed in or applicable to the springing of an iron bar more effective. It is this "peaning" process that splits down the sides of the T rails, and not the weight of machinery. The constant action on the surface of the rail, expands it, tending to make the head wider, but as it does not penetrate sufficiently to spread the whole mass alike, the thin affected portion is forced to crawl over the side of the rail head, and unless it laminates, and thus obtains relief, it often splits the rail down through the sides of the head. All this is visible to every observer, and it will be found more frequently upon the *outer* side of the rail, where there is no contact with the wheels.

The expectations that the cap would grow tighter by this process, has been abundantly justified by experience. Almost the first rails made were put down in March, 1867, upon a branch of the Pennsylvania Central Rail Road, at Johnstown, Pa. Upon some of them (twenty-eight feet long) the cap was purposely left loose, in order to test the above theory. The steel caps not being quite closed in at the sides, were so loose that they could be easily driven off endwise with a hammer. The rails were placed where frequent and heavy trains were passing over them. The result in every case was the same. The cap would at first be moved upon the rail at every passage of the train, in either direction, until it struck the next rail. This continued for a few days, but abated by degrees, until in three weeks, the movement ceased, and the cap began to clinch the iron head, first at the ends and then towards the centre, until in about ninety days the entire rail became as firm, and apparently as solid, as if made of a single piece. A hammer striking the head, would rebound with the same reaction as from a solid mass. Other rails were also laid with the cap originally tight, and the result was equally satisfactory.

Since this first trial the same experiment has been so frequently and thoroughly tried, with the same result, that it has ceased to be a matter of doubt or discussion. *It is settled as conclusively as experience can demonstrate anything, that the cap becomes not looser, but tighter by use.* For additional evidence upon this point, we refer to R. N. Brown, Superindent B. & E. R. R., and T. J. Tillinghast, Superintendent of N. Y. Central, of Buffalo, N. Y., the Booth rail being down upon both roads.

End Movement of Cap.

The apprehension has been expressed that the steel cap would have a tendency to crawl upon the iron, especially upon double track roads, where all trains are passing in one direction. No such movement has ever been discovered in practice, nor can we believe that there is the least reason to expect it. But to render even the fear of it impossible, the iron base of the rail is so rolled, that the iron head on both sides is compressed just below its widest part 1-32 of an inch once in three feet, or at every revolution of the rolls. These deviations or depressions are not abrupt, but commence and end in every three feet, and form, when the steel cap has been firmly secured in its place, an effectual preventive of all possibility of end movement, yet constitute no obstacle to the slight change caused by difference of metallic expansion and contraction.

Practical Results of Eighteen Months' Experience.

This duplex rail has not, as yet, been extensively used. As before stated, a few tons were made in the spring of 1867, at the iron works of the Cambria Iron Company, situated at Johnstown, Penn. They were made with but limited facilities of power and machinery. The only object of their construction was to secure a small number to test the correctness of the inventor's theory, that the loose cap would become tighter by increasing use. The result of the experiment has already been detailed.

One of these rails was laid in the spring of 1867, in the yard of the Buffalo and Erie Rail Road, at Buffalo, under the direction of Mr. R. N. Brown, the Superintendent of the Company. Seventy-five engines, with trains attached, have passed over it daily, in all 40,000 engines and 400,000 cars, and it is to-day as good and firm as when first laid. The iron rails adjoining have been, since the laying of this rail, six times replaced. We have Mr. Brown's letter, stating these facts, and also other letters testifying in the strongest terms to the merits of this rail. We forbear to print them, because of the general impression that it is very easy to procure letters or certificates commendatory of a *new thing*, yet cannot but comment upon the almost universal reluctance of Superintendents and other officers of Rail Road Companies, to recommend a new rail or any improvement of equal importance.

Two of the rails were also laid on the New York Central Rail Road, at Rochester, N. Y., June 7th, 1867. On one the cap was loose and even rattling; on the other it was firm. They were laid continuously, and with the old style of chairs. They were placed where seventy engines and trains daily passed over them on the main line, and where the track was used constantly for switching and making up of trains. The rate of speed over them varies. The through freight trains are frequently joined at this point, three or four in one, to ascend an up grade. They pass over these rails often at the rate of twenty-five or thirty miles an hour. The loose cap rail became tight in a very short time, and both are now in perfect order. Four sets of iron rails have been completely worn out, and new sets replaced on the opposite side of the track, during the period of time these duplex rails have been down.

The practical results of these eighteen months of severe use, including periods of the most extreme cold and the most intense heat to which our climate is liable, apparently settle the question that our method of fastening steel to an iron rail, secures all the elements of safety, durability and economy, and that we have a rail which is, and must continue to be, invaluable.

Oct. 10, 1868. More than a mile of the New York Central Rail Road track, on the main line, just east of Rochester, has been laid with this rail, which point is pronounced by the employees, the hardest mile of main track on the Road—four sets of entire new iron rails have been worn out there in twelve years, in addition to the occasional removal of scattering rails. The grade is here descending eastward, and trains run at full speed. This track is worthy of inspection, and it is claimed that it corroborates all that has so far been promised for this rail.

Smaller quantities have been laid on the same Road, near *Albany;* also on the New York and New Haven Road; on the Cleveland, C. & C. Road, and Chicago & Rock Island Road.

This rail is made for the fish joint, and the tread surface remaining unimpaired, secures substantially a continuous rail.

Thus far no attempt has been made to deviate from the long established form or plan of a rail. We have ventured upon no experiment beyond that necessary to attain perfect security, and in this we believe success has been reached. Should experience determine it to be more advantageous to use a heavier base piece of iron, or a thicker cap of steel, or should these changes, for any special reason, be at any time desired, the requisite alteration can easily be made.

J. L. Booth & Co., have, at Rochester, N. Y., a manufactory established for rolling the steel upon the iron, and furnishing the rail for use. They are now filling an order for the New York Central Road, and will cheerfully show and explain their operations to any person who is interested to call.

October 21st, 1868.

J. L. BOOTH,
Inventor and Patentee,
ROCHESTER, N. Y.

www.ingramcontent.com/pod-product-compliance
Lightning Source LLC
LaVergne TN
LVHW020637110826
845149LV00004B/1236

* 9 7 8 1 4 1 8 1 9 1 3 0 6 *